Characters of Headley's Past

I0162027

Characters

of

Headley's Past

Compiled by
John Owen Smith

Characters of Headley's Past
First published 2017

Typeset and published by John Owen Smith
19 Kay Crescent, Headley Down, Hampshire GU35 8AH

Tel: 01428 712892
wordsmith@johnowensmith.co.uk
www.johnowensmith.co.uk/

© John Owen Smith 2017

All rights reserved. No part of this publication may be reproduced by any means, electronic or mechanical, including photocopy or any information storage and retrieval system without permission in writing from the publisher.

ISBN 978-1-873855-68-3

Printed by CreateSpace

Publisher's Note

This is the second publication to illustrate the history of the parish of Headley.

In the first book, *Headley's Past in Pictures*, we took you on an illustrated tour of the parish as it was during the first half of the 20th century.

Here we look at some of the personalities, groups, occupations and businesses of the past which have helped to create the Headley of today.

Further information on the history of Headley may be found on the Internet at website www.headley-village.com/history

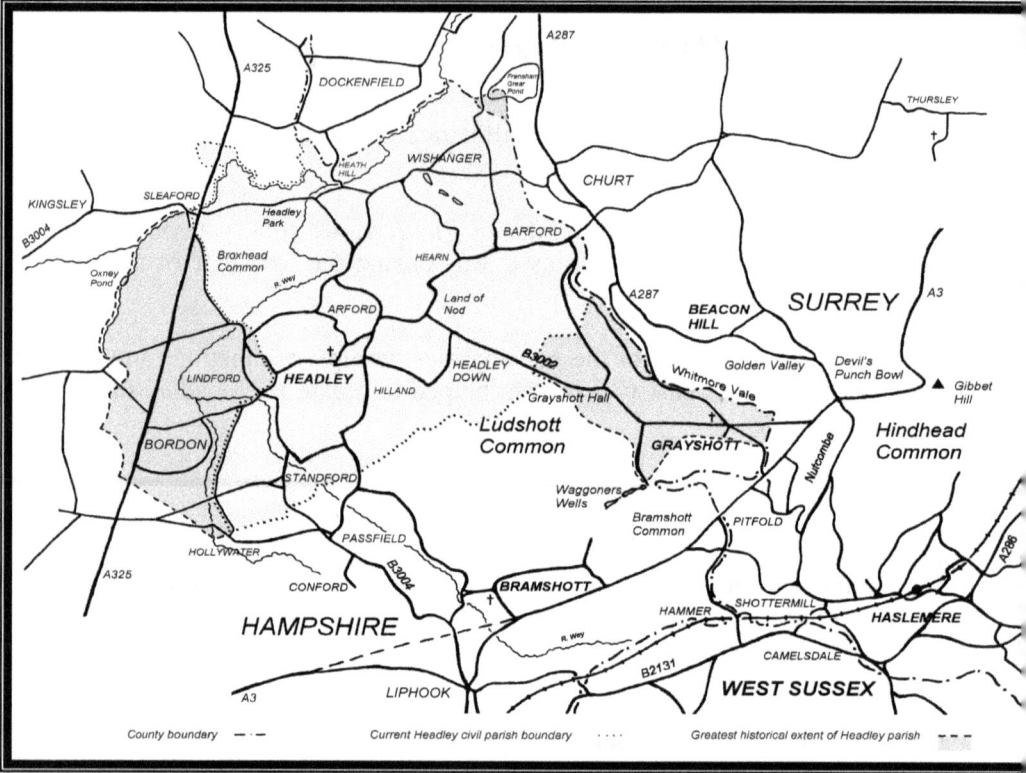

The map shows labels including:

A287, DOCKENFIELD, Frensham Great Pond, THURSLEY, A325, KINGSLEY, SLEAFORD, HEATH HILL, WISHANGER, CHURT, Headley Park, B3004, Braxhead Common, HEARN, BARFORD, Oxney Pond, R. Wey, Land of Nod, A287, BEACON HILL, SURREY, A3, ARFORD, HEADLEY DOWN, B3002, Golden Valley, Devil's Punch Bowl, LINDFORD, HEADLEY, HILLAND, Grayshott Hall, Whitmore Vale, Gibbet Hill, BORDON, Lúdshott Common, GRAYSHOTT, Hindhead Common, STANDFORD, Waggoners Wells, Nutcombe, A286, Bramshott Common, PITFOLD, HOLLYWATER, PASSFIELD, B3004, A325, CONFORD, BRAMSHOTT, HAMMER, SHOTTERMILL, HASLEMERE, HAMPSHIRE, R. Wey, CAMELSDALE, B2131, WEST SUSSEX, A3, LIPHOOK

County boundary — · — Current Headley civil parish boundary · · · · Greatest historical extent of Headley parish – – –

The parish of Headley, showing today's civil parish (light shading), and the greatest extent of the parish as it was up until the start of the 20th century (darker shading).

In 1902, Grayshott became an independent parish; in 1929, the parish of Whitehill was formed taking away Bordon and Lindford; and in 1991, the south bank of Frensham Great Pond became part of Surrey.

Contents

ରେ ରେ ରେ

Joyce Stevens (1914–2007)

Joyce Stevens (née Suter) was born in the village, and educated at the Holme School where her uncle Mr Amos (p.57) was the headmaster, and then at Eggars Grammar School in Alton. She also took to teaching.

She met her husband-to-be in Headley – Robert Plowden Weston Stevens (p.57) who was a young teacher at the Holme School – but by the time they married in April 1942 he had joined the Royal Air Force. Tragically he was killed eight months later in a flying accident in South Africa.

Joyce never remarried, but determined to support herself she completed her degree, became Head of the English Department in Woolmer Hill School, and made teaching her life career.

She took an active role in community life in Headley, being Chairman of Headley Parish Council for five years from 1973 to 1978. She was also one of the first Governors of Alton College.

In 1985 she founded The Headley Society, 'established for the public benefit and interest in the area comprising the civil Parish of Headley and the neighbourhood'. At the time she was advised that her plan to have monthly meetings with an invited speaker at each would not last more than a few months – but it is still going strong today.

Introduction

❧ ❧ ❧

This book is dedicated to Joyce Stevens, a life-time Headley resident, and an inspiration to the rest of us who love the village and strive to record its history.

Every village has had its 'characters', and Headley is no different. But the title of this book is not meant to imply that all who are included here were exceptional. It's true, some found fame beyond the bounds of the parish – however, by and large, this book shows ordinary people going about their everyday lives in a typical English village.

I had promised this book as a follow-up to *Headley's Past in Pictures* which I published in 1999 – eighteen years ago. What took me so long?

In designing the book I was faced with a dilemma – I had many pictures of certain subjects but few of others, and I wanted to produce a book which gave a balanced view of the many different people and organisations which went to form the heart and soul of the village we see today.

I also had to decide what represented the 'Past'. Photographs of recent years are more plentiful, and generally of better quality, than those of more distant times – but their day will come. In my mind I worked to an arbitrary cut-off near the end of the 20th century. This has not always worked, but to me the 'feel' of the selection seems about right.

But the chief delay has been in convincing myself that I'd collected as much information about the people depicted as I could – and of course you never do stop reflecting that there is perhaps a bit more to come. However, time moves inexorably on and with each year there are sadly fewer people to ask.

So here I offer you a selection which I hope you will find fascinating and informative. And if you do have anything you can add, please let me know.

John Owen Smith
Headley 2017

CHURCHES

All Saints Church, Headley, 1903.
Photograph by George Kennett (p.80)

From Kelly's Directory of 1915:—

"The church of All Saints is an edifice of stone in the Decorated style, consisting of chancel, nave, south porch, vestry and a square tower containing 2 bells: the walls were rebuilt and the chancel and vestry added in 1859; the stained east window is a memorial to the Rev Joseph Ballantine Dykes MA, rector 1848 until his death on 28 March 1872; a new organ costing about £300 was placed in the church in 1885; there are 350 sittings.

"The register dates from the year 1538. The living is a rectory, net yearly value £430 with residence, in the gift of the Provost and Fellows of Queen's College, Oxford, and held since 1872 by the Rev Wallis Hay Laverty MA and late fellow of that college.

"In the village is a Congregational chapel erected in 1867 with 200 sittings, and at Lindford a United Methodist chapel holding 200 persons; at Standford is a United Methodist chapel and an iron chapel for the brethren, and at Deadwater Hill a gospel hall."

Joseph Ballantine Dykes, rector 1848–1872

Mr Dykes was a Cumbrian from near Cockermouth. He largely altered the Church after the fire of 1836, building a new Porch, rebuilding the walls, raising the floor nearly 3 feet and adding the Chancel and a Vestry. He also added half an acre to the churchyard in 1868, and enlarged the Holme School by adding a room there in 1871. He died on the evening before Good Friday 1872. He is buried in the churchyard (Plot U9) near to the door to the vestry. In 1874 the East Window was erected in his memory.

Wallis Hay Laverty, rector 1872–1928
Aged 25 on his graduation from Oxford, 1872

"This brilliant young mathematical Fellow of Queen's wanted to get married when it was not permitted, and therefore decided to be ordained. He had no vocation in the ordinary sense, but he was intensely conscientious." *[Headley 1066–1966]*

Married 12th June 1872 to Bessie Geraldine Delamotte, he also published in that year a mathematical treatise *Examples of Conics & Curves*.

He was rector of Headley for the next 56 years until his death.

The Laverty family in the conservatory of the rectory:
L to R: Cecil, Gladys, WHL, Bessie

This picture was taken in 1908 by their elder daughter Muriel, just before their son Cecil emigrated, first to America, then to Australia where he died in 1955. We believe he married there, but have no record of any offspring. Neither Muriel nor Gladys married – both died in Headley in the 1960s.

Muriel Laverty
(1873–1960)
in 1893

Gladys Laverty
(1886–1962)
in 1896

Cecil Laverty
(1877–1955)
in 1880

WH Laverty, Muriel Laverty
Ellen Delamotte, Bessie Laverty, Evelyn Goode
Gladys Laverty, Beryl Goode

Mr Laverty's mother-in-law, Ellen Maria Delamotte, widow of Philip Henry Delamotte, an artist and photographer famous for his images of the dismantling and reassembly of The Crystal Palace 1852–1854.

Bessie Laverty and passenger on a visit.

Bessie Laverty and Reuben Cover, gardener at the Rectory.
He died in 1903 aged 75.

Sunday School Class, April 1901 [from Muriel Laverty's album]:
Nellie Hayden, Kate Dee, Jemima Foard,
Nellie Glaysher, Annie Shrubb, Minnie Gauntlett.

Canon James Spencer Tudor Jones, rector 1934–1966.
On retirement he wrote 'Headley 1066–1966'

The Choir – Top: Mr Nice, ?, visiting soldier?, ?, ?, ?, ?, ?, Ted Warner;
Middle: Mrs Flo Nice, Edna Gamblen, Mr Horniblow, JSTJ, Katie Warner,
Joyce Stevens.   Bottom: John & Peter Gates (twins – not sure which).

Canon Tudor Jones dedicating the new lych gate in May 1954 erected to commemorate the Queen's Coronation.

The congregation entering through the gate. Some members identified: Mrs Bellinger (hat & glasses at front), Mr Robinson (bald, far left), Dorothy Ellis (to right of gate), Mr & Mrs Allden, Mrs Tudor Jones (mid-right), Reg, Nancy & Susan Thackeray (on far right)

19

*David Edward Bentley, rector 1966–1974, wearing the Headley Cope
on its dedication at All Saints Church on 28th May 1972.
Made from material intended for the wedding dress of 19-year old Tamara
Ashmore, who was killed in the Hither Green train crash of November 1967.*

Chapel at Barford, by the bridge – photo of Sunday School in early 1900s.
Nigel Thorne's aunt Lillie went there. It closed around 1930.

Construction of St Luke's, Grayshott c.1898. Picture from Ron Caswell
whose grandfather James J Beard was a master carpenter there.

Many Lithuanians from Headley Park
have been buried in All Saints churchyard.

HEADLEY PARK

a short history

1555	Heath House first mentioned in the Parish Registers, in the Manor of Broxhead (became Headley Park).
1618–late 1600s	John Fauntleroy, bapt 1588 Crondall; moved to Heath House, Headley 1618; buried in Headley Nov 1644.
	His son Moore Fauntleroy emigrated to Virginia 1643; d. 1663.
1700s	Huggins/Gatehouse/Blunt family:
	1727 John Huggins lived at Heath House; 1747 Thomas Gatehouse Jnr Esq, married Ann Maria Huggins, eldest daughter of Wm Huggins; 1761 Anna inherits Heath House on father's death; her daughter Mrs Blunt inherits from her. Sold by family c.1820?
1800s	The old house is said to have been destroyed, perhaps in the great common fire of 1864.
1871–Oct 1888	Heath House (Headley Park) bought by The Hon. Sir Henry Singer Keating, celebrated Victorian judge, from William Langrish 28th February 1871; Sir Henry retired in January 1875.
1884	New house built 'positioned to view the Hindhead hills' in place of the old Heath House.
c.1890–1904	Sir Robert Wright, Justice of the High Court
1904–1947	Charles McAndrew, who owned a shipping line later taken over by P&O. The McAndrew family left Headley Park after WW2 because the course of the river altered and affected their supply of electricity and water.
1947–1955	Crusaders' Preparatory School.
1955–2014	"Lietuviu Sodyba" or "Lithuanians' Homestead" called 'Headley Park Hotel', closed November 2014.
2017	An application was made to redevelop the site.

John Huggins 1655-1745.
Solicitor, member of the Middle
Temple & High Bailiff of
Westminster – father of William.
Bought Headley Park 1727

William Huggins 1696–1761.
Friend of Tobias Smollett &
William Hogarth: 'His genius was
so happy, quick and versatile that
he easily acquired whatever befits
a scholar and a gentleman.'

Mr and Mrs Blunt

She was g/daughter of William
Huggins and inherited the house

Sir Robert wrote a number of books on classic literature and legal matters, including an essay on possession in the common law (1888) with Sir Frederick Pollock who lived at Hindhead at the time.

Soon after that, the Wrights moved to Headley Park.

Devastated by the death of their young son Evan Stanley (Master Jack) in 1900, the Wrights installed the clock on All Saints Church tower in his memory.

Sir Robert Samuel Wright
1839–1904

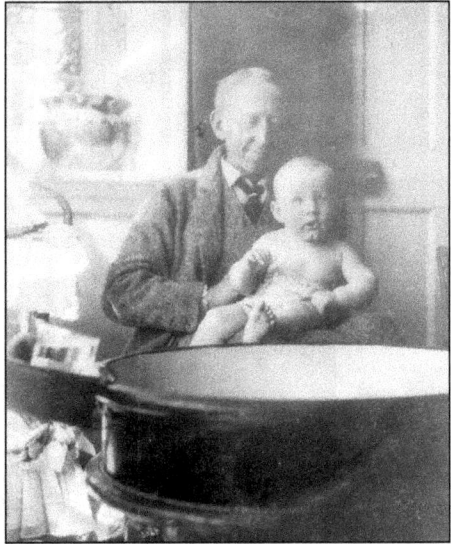

The Wrights with Jack, b.1893
d.13 Jan 1900 age 6, of influenza

25

Mr & Mrs MacAndrew at Headley Park – October 1918

*Mrs Patsy McAndrew (later Mrs Barnard) and her daughter Caroline
in Headley Park library, 1946*

BUSINESSES

In Headley, as in most villages, there were many small businesses set up to cater for local needs at a time when travelling to the market towns was not easy or convenient.

Gradually the advent of easier travel killed off the demand for them, and in Arford in particular there are now no shops where there used to be several.

In the following pages we show some of the people who catered for the villagers' needs in days past.

Said to be the ford at Headley Mill in 1901
the picture shows a pace of business activity different from today.

[Mr Laverty's collection]

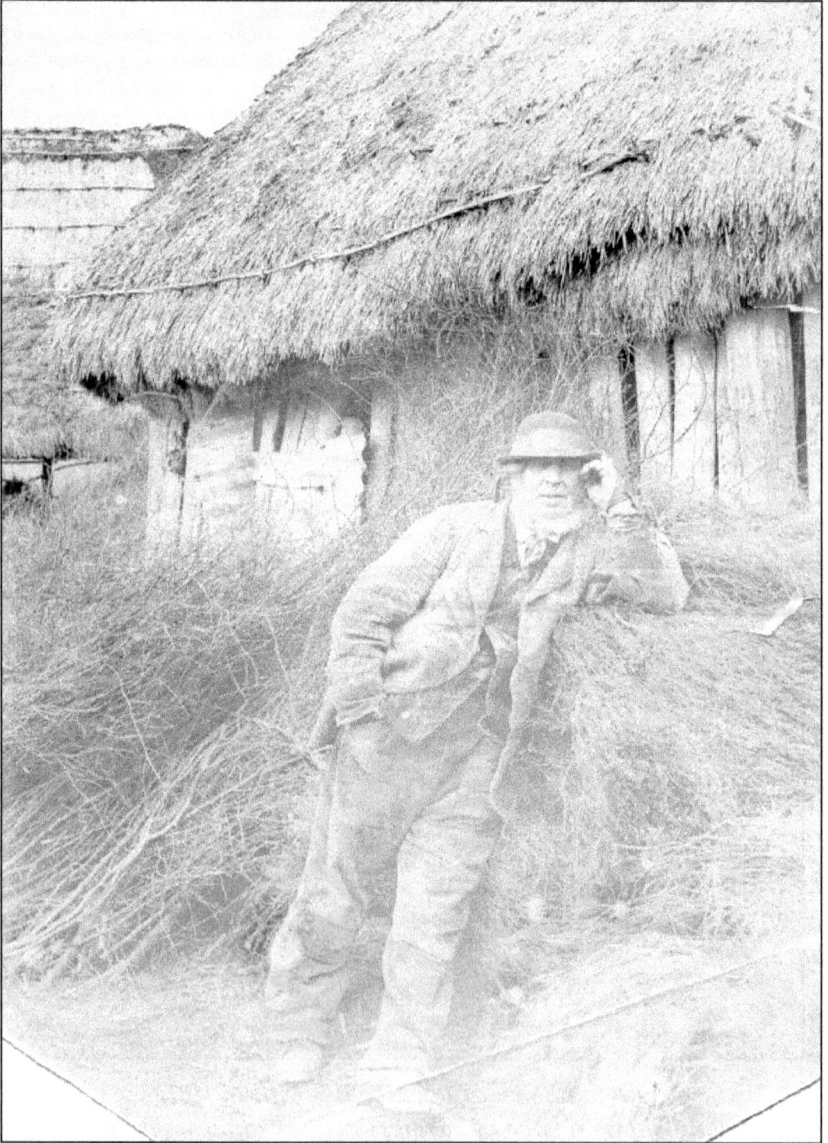

Edward Coombes, broom-squire – died 30 Sep 1899
– photographed near his cottage on Arford Common
– he sold brooms for 3/- per dozen at Farnham market

Archie Bellinger 'had a fine tenor voice
and sang in the church choir for many years'

In 1913 began the reign (to 1958) of the Bellinger family at the Arford Up to
Date Stores, *a title which caused much merriment among the Canadians*
stationed here during WW2. It became a typical village store, selling
"anything from dolls' eyes to railway arches", as the old saying goes.

THE STORES. CHURCH GATE, HEADLEY.

Headley School Trustees

Bought of CURTIS BROTHERS,

DRAPERS, SILK MERCERS, UPHOLSTERERS,

Complete House Furnishers, &c.

Hosiery	Dresses	Millinery	Ready Mades
Gloves	Costumes, Silks	Mantles	Tailoring
Ribbons	Household Linen	Straws	Boots and Shoes
Lace	Muslins	Carpets	Hats and Caps
Trimmings	Stays	Furniture	Paper Hangings
Haberdashery	Underclothing	Bedsteads	Bedding, etc . etc.

Family Mourning.

MUSICAL INSTRUMENTS OF EVERY DESCRIPTION.

CASH ON OR BEFORE DELIVERY.

ON WEDNESDAYS AT TWO

16.	Paper	4½	6	0
9	do	6	4	6
12	do	6½	6	6
8	do	5	3	4
			1 . 0	. 4

Invoice dated 1902 from Curtis Bros Stores at Churchgate.
Run by Richard & George Curtis, no relation to James (next page).

James Curtis in his 92nd year, July 1916 – he died 24th Nov 1916.
Kept shop opposite the Wheatsheaf in Arford, later Bohanna's.

The Headley Restaurant in Long Cross Hill.
Probably early 1900s.

Bob Tidey the baker in Headley High Street c.1906.
Photograph by George Kennett (p.80)

A mixed group outside the Crown Inn, Arford.
Local baker, Bob Tidey, on horse.
Holroyd & Healy's Breweries Ltd existed from the late 1890s to 1956.

Miss Stenning outside her shop in Arford.

A wooden building, this became a little general shop after the original owners died. Miss Stenning, whose brother was a baker, sold bread and cakes, confectionery, cigarettes, haberdashery, toys and newspapers. *Apple Tree* now occupies the site. [Joyce Stevens, *To the Ar and Back*]

Rogers' Stores in the 1950s.

Beatrice & Leonard (Beattie & Len) Rogers at the back of their shop.

'Headley Stores' was run by William Rogers from 1895; his children, Len and Beattie, later ran it until she died, then it began to go downhill. Len carried on alone, living in one room in cold and discomfort. Finally, in 1957, being persuaded to sell much against his will, he took out his ancient gun and killed himself. [Joyce Stevens, *To the Ar and Back*]

Jonas Shrubb ran a grocer's shop in Hammer Lane, Barford. In 1881 he was 'summoned for having a scale in his possession 3½oz short' – fined 15s. [Newspaper cutting from WH Laverty's notes]

Bread delivery from Hammer Lane driven by Monty Mullard prior to 1914.

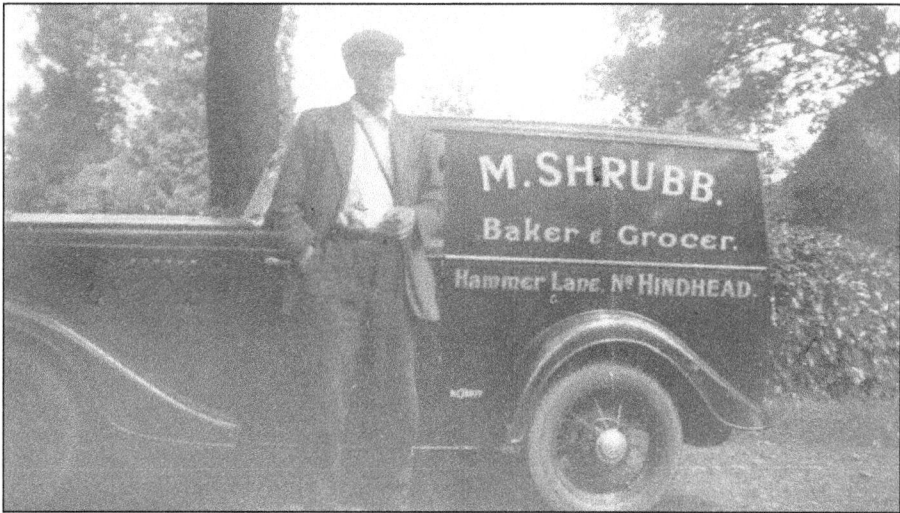

Bread delivery from Hammer Lane driven by Percy Young circa 1950.

White House Dairy, Headley High Street in the 1950s.

*Headley High Street in 1965. Today a parade of three shops,
but the phone box is still there, now housing a defibrillator!*

Probably Frederick & John Lickfold
who ran a cycle shop at Headley Mill in the early 1900s

Joyce Stevens' father, Percy Suter at the wheel with one of the Lickfold
brothers outside their cycle shop at Headley Mill, c.1903.

Delivering 'farmers grist' to Headley Mill c.1930.
This was 'rough ground' and returned to the farmer for animal feed.

Unloading bran at Headley Mill c.1930.
Peter Ellis on the lorry. His father Frederick unloading the sacks.

Left: delivery van belonging to J. Ellis of Headley Mill.
Right: delivery lorry belonging to J. Ellis's brother.
Peter Ellis's sister behind. [Information Peter Ellis, June 2001]

Aerial view of Headley Mill in 1955.

Aerial view of Whittles Stores, Headley Down in 1964.
The pitched roofs of the original laundry can be seen
at an angle to the front of the shop, which closed in 2015.

View south-east from All Saints Church tower in the 1960s.
Note businesses in the High Street: Churchgate Stores (rear of); Holly Bush;
Bargrave Deane (was Rogers); Wakeford (butcher); & NatWest Bank.
Also see Tonards Garage on Crabtree Lane.

Hop picking near Headley – date & location unknown

Hops were an important local crop. It was noted, for example, that Mr Justice Wright of Headley Park (p.25) "gave over a considerable acreage to hop cultivation, to provide local employment."

Somebody has been indicated with a white 'X', in the lower photograph but sadly we don't know who it is.

The Ancient Order of Foresters was a mutual organisation caring for the sick. Court "Forget-me-not" was founded in Headley in 1882.

Front and back of the Foresters' banner held in Headley Archives.

ORGANISATIONS

The Foresters' marching band at the 1906 Fete

Several village organisations were founded in Mr Laverty's time: for example the cricket & football clubs and the Horticultural Society. Some still exist but others, like the Foresters and its brass band shown here, are no longer with us.

Since then other organisations have been formed, and in these next few pages we show you a selection of pictures of some of them drawn from the village archives.

Other pictures are shown in the 'Pageants & Drama' and 'Sports' sections.

And we are happy to report that a healthy number of organisations are alive and well in and around Headley today. At a "Here's Headley" weekend in 2015, organised by The Headley Society, there were over 40 local organisations vying for residents' attention.

Mr Wakeford with a charabanc party from Headley.
Date and location unknown. He was the butcher in Headley.
[From his granddaughter Rita Beaven, née Wakeford]

Baby Welfare Group outside Headley Village Hall
– late 1920s, soon after the hall was built in 1925.

Bordon Drag Hounds on Headley Village Green
run by Quavers? in Bordon in early 1930s.
Master: Capt Selby-Lowndes RA
[Photo given by Mrs Downing]

A fine picture from our archives, but we have no idea who these men are.
Can you help us identify them?

Youth Fellowship Group – mid 1940s.

Back L to R: ? Brooker, –, John White, Angela Hack, Joyce Read, ? White,
Jill Woodford, Jean Radford, Don Walsh, Lily Fisher, Doris Kelly,
? Brooker, –, Rosemary Hooker, Mary Woodger (Williams), Don Parfect.
Middle: Bob Toovey, Alan 'Ginger' Gandy, Ray Harris, Phyllis Read,
Joyce Hedgecock, ? Clark, Eileen Cummins, Ted Smith?, ? Read,
Dennis Fisher, Pat Edwards, Bob Willis, –.
Front: ? Tribe, –, Barbara Tudor Jones, John George?, Joyce Stevens,
Rev Tudor Jones, Elsie Earl (Watkins), Peter Ellis, Joyce Lamberton,
Joy Billiat.
Squatting: David Whittle, Jean Allen.

Banquet of Youth Fellowship Group (1948-49).

Standing L to R: Pamela Coombes, Donald Parfect, Jean Radford,
Cissy Blacklaws, Ethel Warriker.
Back seated L to R: Elsie Earl, Jimmy White, –, Phyllis Allen, –,
Kathleen Amey, Donald Walsh, gap, Dennis Woodger, Gloria Houlin,
John Courtnage.
Front L to R: Lorraine Hack, John Heather, Mary Courtnage,
Leonard Hack, , –, Kathleen Toovey.

Cubs during World War 2

Cubs starting 27 May 1939: John Power, Robert Toovey, Billy Worman, Raymond Holloway, Peter Woodford, John Warner.

Saying goodbye to Bagheera (Miss Laurie) – 15th June 1940
Back: Bob West, John White, Bagheera, Baloo (Joyce Suter), John Statham;
Front: George Ralph, Bob Toovey, Raymond Holloway, Alan Witte.

June 1941, possibly at Follyfield: G Cooke, Bagheera, Akela,
B Innes, B Toovey, D Parfitt?, B Warner, D Young.

The Pack, April 1941 – Blacks: D Young, J White (Snowball), A Witte,
B Toovey, J Power, J Warner, J White. Greys: A Gandy (Ginger), B Innes,
J Legat, J Cooke, P Davis, Jim White, J Statham.

A children's party in Headley – details unknown

Members and wives of the Headley and District branch of the British Legion at their annual dinner, 20th February 1954.
Top row: *Mrs Eames, Mrs Caswell, Mr Caswell, Mr Dean, Mrs Dean, Mr North, Mrs Ridgeway and two guests from the Grayshott branch.* ***Bottom:*** *Jim Wakeford, Mrs Leggett, Mr Merrit, Mr & Mrs de Bate, Mr Leggett.*

Brownies in the 1980s

Headley Brownies & leaders on Pack Holiday in 1985.

Headley Brownies in fancy dress for Guy Fawkes Night, c.1989.

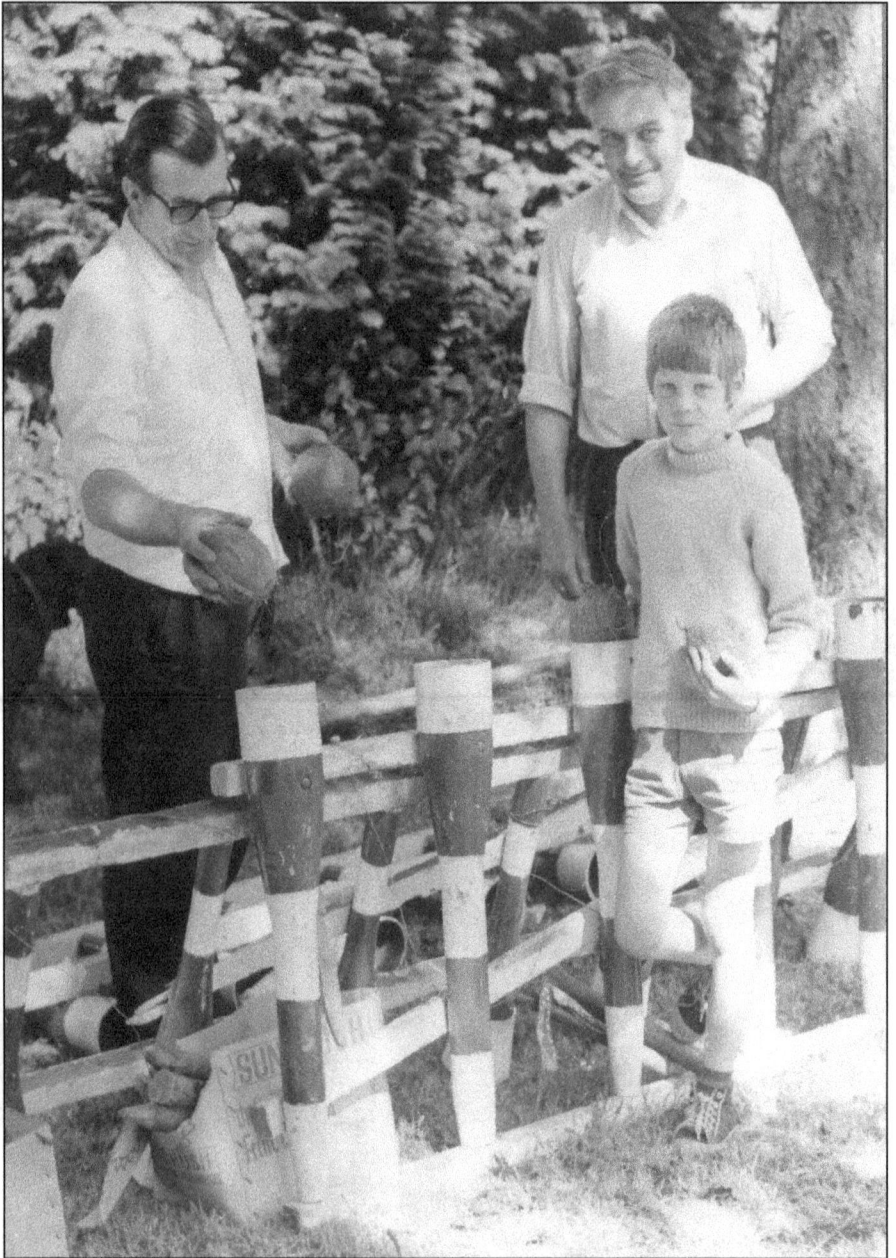

*Mr W Applebee, chairman of the Headley Down Playing Field Association,
sets up a coconut shy at the association's fete on Saturday, with Mr John
Eames, a member of the committee, and eight-year-old Peter Coucher.
[The Herald, Friday 6th July 1973]*

THE HOLME SCHOOL

In 1755 George Holme, Doctor of Divinity and rector of Headley, petitioned the Bishop of Winchester as follows:—

"Herewith that your petitioner hath for several years set up a Charity School in the said parish of Hedley the greatest part of which lies within your Lordship's said Manor of Bishops Sutton, And your petitioner intends to make provision for the perpetual endowment of the said school and to be at the expense of building a new school and a dwelling house, garden and other conveniences for the Master.

"That your petitioner hath not of his own a piece of ground properly situated for such intended building and conveniences, but there is a small piece or parcel of your Lordship's Waste containing by estimation half an acre, abutting to the west on the Glebe lands belonging to your petitioner as Rector aforesaid, and to the south east and north parts another part of the said Waste, which lies very convenient for that purpose — on which piece of ground your petitioner is desirous of erecting his intended buildings if he can obtain a grant thereof from your Lordships — Your petitioner therefore humbly prays your Lordships to order your Steward at the next court to be holden for the said Manor to make a copyhold grant to your petitioner and his heirs or to such persons as he shall direct for the purpose aforesaid of the said piece of Waste ground, under such small fine and rent as shall be thought reasonable. And your petitioner shall ever pray, etc. — George Holme, March 4, 1755."

To which was added:—
"I consent to what is requested in this petition — B. Winchester."

And so a double-fronted structure comprising school and Master's house was built at the side of what is now the village green – and is still there today, though no longer used as a school.

The Foundation Deed stated that the children were to be educated "in such principles of learning and knowledge as are most proper for such young persons, that is to say, the boys in Reading, Writing and Common Arithmetic, and the girls in Reading, Writing & Arithmetic and in Sewing and Knitting."

Also: "The school is to consist of 1 master and any number of children, but only 12 shall be upon the charity. In choosing the 12 children to be educated free, preference is to be given to children of the poor inhabitants of Headley, and the number filled up from the like of Bramshott and Kingsley."

Holme School children in 1896.

Holme School children – date unknown

Holme School children in 1920 on Bramshott Chase
Mrs Beck on left, Miss Christian on right.
Joyce Suter (Stevens) is 5th child from right in top row.

Holme School children in 1922.
Top: *?, Roy Dyer, ?, Bob Stevens, ?, ?, Billy Brown.* **Third row:** *Alice Coombs, Thelma Pavitt, Edith Smith, Kitty Libretto, Ethel Sawkins, Phyllis Turner, Hilda Chappell, Dorothy Figg.* **Second row:** *Maidie Smith, Peggy Hack, Nellie Denyer, Cissy White (with slate), Edith Maidwell, Joyce Suter (Stevens), Phillis Dowler.* **Bottom:** *Charlie Hall, William Kilburn, Roy Coombs, Norman Deane, Harold Glaysher.*

[Names supplied by Joyce Stevens]

55

Holme School teams in 1932 when the school won the area shield for sports.
Girls won the cup for netball; boys the football shield.
Mr Amos (head) on the left, Miss Hall (headmistress) on right.
Top: *?, ?, Bill McCardle, Dennis Dean, Victoria Smith, ?, Elizabeth Wells.*
Middle: *Elsie Marshall, Ted Chesham, Percy Woodger, ?, Vera Chiverton*
(holding cup), Gerald Kemp (holding large shield), Heather Hack, ?.
Front: *?, ?, Peggy Franklin, Basil Fyfield, ?Stoneman, ?.*

Holme School stoolball team, 1934.

Holme School children in 1936.

Top: *Mollie Small, ?, Pearl Small, ?, Alice Fyfield, ?, Susan Lamport, Joyce Marshall, Hazel Hack, Una Putnam, Freda Putnam.*

Third row: *Ken Hunt, John Whittle, Arthur Dean, Frank Woodger, Aubrey Hack, ?, Fred Caswell, Fred Woodger, Ernie Warwick, John Coombes, Bernard Marshall.*

Second row: *Mr Amos, Rendall Read, Arthur Hodgton, Joe North, Bert Caswell, ?, Harry Fisher, Joe Gatcum, ?, ?, John Willis, Mr RPW Stevens.*

Bottom: *Gladys Hannon, Pat Gamblen, Nell Coombes, Phyllis Hudson, ?, ?, Nancy Smith, Pam White, Betty Aldred, J & L Caldicots, Rosie Moss.*

[Information: Mr F Woodger]

A school play, date unknown

57

Holme School Cricket Team 1948.
Back*: Taylor, Len Hack, Ken Sharman, Wally Courtnage, John Blacklaws,
Tony Gates. **Middle row**: Dennis Woodger, Jim Passingham, Wally North,
Cliff Blanchard, Billy Gatcum. **Bottom**: Andy McGorgan, Cyril Willis,
Andy Gandy, Brian Hudson, Philip Courtnage.
[Information: Michael Aldred]*

Holme School teachers, c.1950.
*Back: Mr John Wiltshire; Mr Edward Lea (headmaster); Mr Geoff Parfitt
Front: Elsie Watkins; Betty Thomas; Mabel Hussey; Mrs Waller
[Information: David Hardy]*

58

L: Mrs Earl (mother of Elsie Watkins) – R: Miss Mabel (Mabs) Hussey, long-serving teacher at Headley Holme school.

Miss Hussey kept a diary from Aug 1940 to July 1941 telling of conditions at the school during those years of WW2.

Her first entry reads: *"Friday 2nd Aug* – Closed school for a curtailed summer holiday of two weeks, owing to the war. Decided to keep a diary."

Other typical entries are:

Tue 20th Aug – Enemy aircraft overhead during afternoon playtime. I had to dive into school shelters with two classes. Luckily we were soon out again.

Fri 29th Aug – Siren went at 11.45am – marshalled our charges to the dugouts – remained there for an hour. School reopened at 2 instead of 1.30. Stevey [Mr RPW Stevens], our Assistant Master, went to Portsmouth for his medical today – passed Grade 1, and is down for the Air Force.

Wed 10th Sep – Siren went at 10.45am – lasted till 11.45 – so not much work done. Siren went again at 3.45 – what a rotten time, just as we were ready to close school – had to stay in the shelters till 5 o'clock. Did I enjoy my cup of tea? I'll say I did!

Wed 18th Sep – I've had several new children recently, bombed out of London I presume. Number on register 48 – far too many.

Mon 13th Jan – My usual luck – Miss Barrow away ill – I have her class to cope with – number on both registers 90 children.

Sun 1st June – What a bombshell in the papers! – clothes rationing!!! Got my leg well pulled for not buying anything while visiting Reading yesterday, being in need of many things. It was a great surprise to us and the secret had been well kept – everybody talking and counting in 'coupons'.

Tue 3rd June – A visit from our Drill Inspectress – seemed thrilled with my squad – so much so that another teacher was invited out to watch.

Her last entry reads: *"Sun 20th July* – Returned to Headley – arrived at Bordon 10.20. Some drunken Canadian vomited all over me in the bus – so the end of a perfect holiday!"

'Gunner' Coombes tosses the bale in a 1950 'Country Fete'
(see him also in the Sports section)

PAGEANTS AND DRAMA

We have in the archives a list of Military Tournaments held on the Rectory Field in association with the annual Summer Flower Show between 1896 and 1905. At that time Bordon was included in Headley parish, and the connection with the Army was strong.

1896 Tournament by the Seaforth Highlanders
1897 Military Tournament by the 3rd (King's Own) Hussars
1898 Royal Dublin Fusiliers display of Physical Drill & Irish Dancing to their band
1899 Musical Ride & Display by 12th (Prince of Wales) Royal Lancers (cancelled – due to Boer War?)
1900 Band of 1st (King's) Dragoon Guards
1901 Band of Queen's Bays
1902 Band of Highland Light Infantry Pipers and Dancing
1904 Military Sports & Band of Wiltshire Regiment
1905 Military Tournament (King's Royal) Irish Hussars

Sadly, we have no pictures of those activities, but pageants, carnivals, fetes, fairs, drama and festivities continued, and continue to be held in the village.

In particular the Pageant of 1951, held to celebrate the Festival of Britain, resulted in the formation of Headley Theatre Club which, in 2017, celebrates its 65th anniversary.

Scene from the pageant of 1951 to celebrate the 'Festival of Britain'
From the success of this, Headley Theatre Club was formed in 1952.

Scene from the pageant of 1953 to celebrate the Coronation.
Episode VI: William & Mary

Both pageants were held in the grounds of Wodehouse, Liphook Road.

1951: Producer Mrs Frances Paton-Hood, & Rector Canon Tudor Jones enjoying the show.

1951 Pageant chorus.
Back row*: Dorothy Clark, June Booley, Gladys Croft, Ann Jewell, Margaret Robbins, Sheila Hunt, Susan Burningham, Glenda Nash, June Able, Ivy Tubb, ?, Freda Taylor, Sheila Walsh, Jean Williamson, Margaret Fisher, Edith Goodyear and Jean Kemp. **Middle row***: P Martin, Jacky Sinclair, June Marshall, Dorothy Keith, Iris Harris, Sally Woodford, Valerie Beecham and Margaret Smith. **Front row***: Diana Smith, Ann North, Patsy Goddard, Mary Fisher, Joyce Hillier, ?, ?, ? Leggett, Jean Tompsett, Valerie Cowie and ?*

*Headley Theatre Club 1955 – 'The Happiest Days of Your Life'
directed by Di Rabbetts.*

*Headley WI in a one-act play in 1972 'They Made Her Wild'
Cast: Esther Lucas, Evelyn Meek, Marie Bryan, Rie Gerstel, Doreen Keen,
Joan Parkinson & Doreen Leighton.*

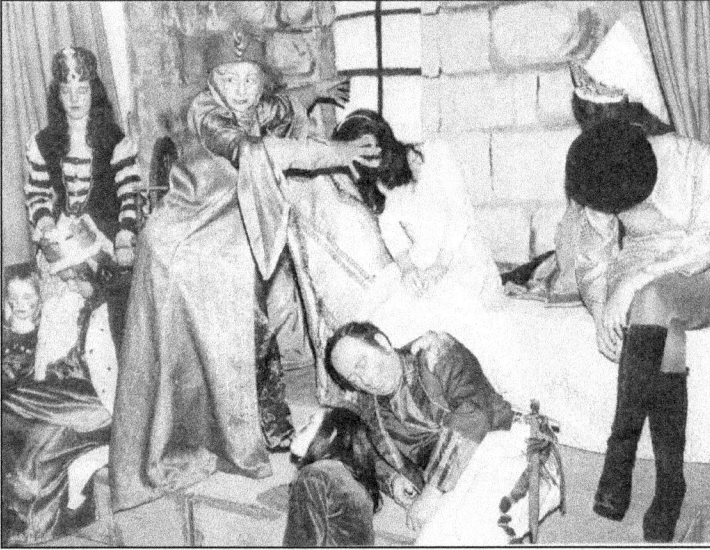

Headley Theatre Club, Jan 1973 'Sleeping Beauty':
Pru Harrold, Phyl Brewster, Vicky Cook, Ray Pascoe.

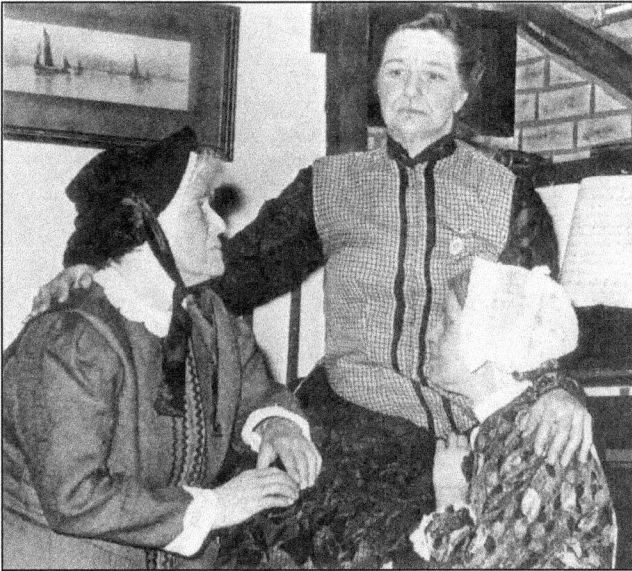

Headley Theatre Club, May 1973 'Ladies in Retirement':
Ellen played by Dawn Lewock, centre, comforts Emily (Rie Gerstel)
on the left, and Louisa (Doreen Keen).

Headley Guides in Churchill Crescent, preparing to march to the Queen's Silver Jubilee celebrations, 1977.

Pearly king and queen at the Queen's Silver Jubilee celebrations, 1977.

Two pictures from Headley's 'Village Day' – 20th June 1998
Parade to the Village Green.

Paul & Carole Burns and Jeremy Whitaker at the Millennium Pageant 10th June 2000.

The Headley Theatre Club float in Churchfields heading for the Village Green and the Millennium Pageant.

SPORT

Ladies' cricket was popular in Victorian times, as the first two pictures in this section show, though how they judged 'leg before wicket' remains a mystery!

The rector's two daughters were in the Headley team, and records from Grayshott show that young ladies of breeding were playing the game with enthusiasm there too.

Headley Cricket Club men's team played its first match on 12th May 1872, Mr Laverty's first year here as rector, and is one of the oldest teams in the district.

In 1901, Edward Blakeway I'Anson offered to give a cup for a cricket competition among the villages surrounding Grayshott, and the I'Anson Competition was born. In his book about the competition 'A Cup for Cricket' Theo Pope writes of Headley: "The Rectory Field on a hot summer's day, with buttercups thick in the outfield and sloping down to the long, rather narrow table in the centre, with the Holme School at the bottom end ... most cricketers who have visited Headley will recall that picture ... and the magnificent horse chestnut on the boundary, a challenge to every hitter."

You can see that tree in the first picture of the ladies' cricket match.

Football and bowls are the other two sports which feature in the following pages, and both, like the cricket, are still going strong today.

Ladies' cricket match on the Rectory Field c.1890.

Headley Ladies Cricket Team, 1897.
Standing: *Mrs Thompson, E[mma] M[ary] Hahn, M[uriel] Laverty, Laura Rogers, Ethel Julius, Marion Smithes, Edith Julius, Mary Macdonald, Mrs Casson, Mrs Miney(?), Mary Hulbert, Mrs Phillips, Miss Thornwaite;*
Sitting: *Con Burgess, Amelia Casson, G[ladys] Laverty, Helen Bewsher, Miss Pullen-Berry(?), Ada Rogers, Miss Miney(?), Miss C Thristram*

The Wednesday Cricket Team c.1906.

Headley 2nd Football Team, 1931-32.
Back row: *E Ashford, T Nelson, F Green, A Croucher, E Arthurs, R Bond,*
T Lemon. **Front row**: *H Chisnall, J Gates, J Chisnall, C Kingswood.*
[Information: J Chisnall]

S. J. (Gunner) Coombes in 1935: 'used his bat like a flail and achieved remarkable results with his tearaway bowling' [A Cup For Cricket, LT Pope]

Note the use of the Rectory Field for cricket matches at this time.

Headley Cricket Club team winners of 1938 I'Anson Cup.
Back row (L to R): HJ Knight (competition Hon Sec), AJ Bellinger,
RPW Stevens, LT Pope, RW Johnstone, T Lemon;
Second row: C Nicholls (umpire), HAP Heslop, F Dopson, J Radford,
J Hudson, W Dunk, W North, A Bellinger (Hon Treas);
Front row: E Turner (Hon Sec), F Courtnage, Capt RH Thackeray, E Nash
(captain), GM Hubbuck, H Blanchard, AJ Stevens (competition president)

Headley Cricket Club team winners of 1962 I'Anson Cup.

Bob White and Frank Kenward with I'Anson Cup in 1962.

"Headley Bowling Club trophy winners, pictured in 1950."
Photograph from the Herald 23 Sept 1988. The line-up is, from the left,
Messrs Green, Colan, Chisnall, Read, Watson and Thackeray."

Probably from the same era: L to R—
Jim Chisnall, Gunner Coombes, Nancy Thackeray, Jim Handy, Mrs Gray,
Reg Thackeray, Ted Warner, Major Billiat.

Different forms of local transport in the past

HEADLEY FAMILIES

Over the years we have received many photographs of old Headley families, several from descendants now living abroad. The following pages show some of these.

Dennis John Chiverton, pulling the flag off the plaque on Headley Village Green, celebrating the jubilee of King George V, 5th May 1935.
He was 6 years old.

Over the years the plaque became detached from its plinth,
and is now on display in the foyer of the Village Hall.

George Frederick & Annie Eliza Kennett.
He had a watchmaker's business in Headley High Street
and was also well-known locally as a keen photographer.

The wedding group for George & Annie's daughter Ida Mildred Kennett
who married John Augustus Carbine, an Australian soldier,
at All Saints, Headley in January 1919.
[Photos from Ian Carbine, grandson of John & Ida]

Joshua Francis & Eliza Harriet Kenward at Glenside, Honeysuckle Lane.
He died in 1962 aged 82; she died in 1982 aged 101.
[Photo from Mrs Plummer (née Kenward)]

William & Nellie Moore. He ran the Wheatsheaf Inn during WW1
and died in 1921. She was a nurse & midwife.
[Photo from Pam Jones, their granddaughter]

Anne Glaysher (b.1829 née North, d.1911) outside her house in Barford.
Married to William in 1852 – he died 1884 aged 60.
Their son James emigrated to America in 1921.
[Photo from her gt-gt-grandson, Fred Glaysher in Michigan, USA]

L to R: Harry Fyfield, ?, ?, Harry Blanchard, ?, ?, Charles Courtnage
Inscription reads 'Headley Rectory 1929'
[Photo from Joan Courtnage]

Fanny Gamblen (b.1848 née Mullins) in 1901, wife of Oscar.
Several members of the Gamblen family lived down Long Cross Hill.

Albert Percy 'Bert' Heather (b.1905) cowman at Long Cross Farm
with Basil Albert Gamblen (b.1922)

Entitled 'The Ladies of Lane End' (at the end of the Headley Fields lane)
Donated to the present occupants by Catherine Willis.
We are not sure who is shown here, but best guess is from the 1911 census:
3 servants: Charles Whipps, his wife and another female servant Nellie Sear.
All were in their mid-20s at the time

Mary Ann Coombes (b.1864 née Burrows, d.1937).
She lived in Arford and had 12 children

Margaret Hack, granddaughter of Mary Ann Coombes.
[Photos from Margaret's granddaughter Sherri]

Taken at Linstead Farm, Headley – possibly 1924-1925.

"My grandmother, Alice Mary Lamport (née Lawes); grandfather, Harry Charles Lamport; uncle Bill, William Richard Lamport; uncle Harry, Harry George Lamport; aunt Sue, Rosemary Lamport; and Rosy the horse."

[Photo & text from Mrs S Pollard of Salisbury]

Wedding of Daphne Phillips to Maj Leonard Robinson, 2 Feb 1921

Waiting for bride & groom in Headley High Street

The happy couple outside Hilland Farm

[Photos from Ron Caswell, whose mother was housekeeper at Hilland]

The Hubbuck family at a picnic, early C20th.
Edward Hubbuck had 'Pinehurst' (now 'Benifold') built in 1899
in Headley Hill Road. He died in Aug 1901.
His wife Harriette lived there until her death in 1935.

Members of the Trollope family outside 'Windridge', 4 Sept 1927.
They lived next door to Mrs Hubbuck (see above)

In the garden of Elmside, Lindford, 1st Sept 1907.
Standing*: Ellen (Nell) Viney (née Rowe), Frank Augustus John Viney,*
Charlotte Viney, John Henry Viney (junior), Emmaline Viney (née Triggs).
Seated*: Sgt Edward Kennett Budd, R.E., Jenetta Adelaide Budd (née Viney),*
sister of Nell, John Henry Viney (senior)

Dressed for the Headley carnival:
John Henry Viney (junior) with
grandsons, Edward (Ted) Budd
(b. Jan 1910), and Jack Leet
(b. May 1912), taken c.1919.

John Henry Viney (junior)
and Emmaline

[Photos from Phil & Ann Viney]

Leo Nicolai outside 'Fellmongers' at the bottom of Beech Hill Road in the 1940s

Victoria Nicolai (née Smith) wife of Leo.
She was born in 1919: they emigrated to the USA in 1952
with their children Michael and Gloria.

[Photos from Michael and Gloria]

*Gloria ('Ginger') and Michael Nicolai
outside 'Fellmongers'*

*George Smith, father of Victoria, aged 90 outside 'Fellmongers'
with his gt-grandson George.*

Wedding of George Barnes to Kate Trussler, 7 June 1913.
Standing: *Flo Trussler, Grace Trussler, Edith Trussler, ?, ?, ?, ?, Ruth Trussler, ?, ?.* **Middle**: *Louisa Trussler (mother), Thomas Trussler (father), Alice Trussler (bridesmaid), Kate Trussler (bride), George Barnes, Bridesmaid, Tom Trussler (brother).* **Front**: *3 boys.*

Henry George & Emily Swayne had children: Arthur George 1892; Fred William 1893; Edw Frank 1895; Elsie 1897; Richard Martin 1899; John 1905. This photo is from Elsie's g/daughter Wendy Buckingham (née Nash) who says that Elsie (not in the picture) moved to Ferndale Terrace c.1922.

90

The Payne family, later of Wey Valley Farm, Standford – in 1910.
Front: Charlie; Centre: Harry and Flora, his father and mother
Back, his brothers and sister: left, George; centre, Nell; right, Fred

[Photo from Charlie's son Denis Payne]

I'ANSON & WHITAKER

Jack Smith, in his book *Grayshott*, said: "Grayshott is a late example of a village growing under the influence of a benevolent autocracy represented, though not exclusively, by the I'Ansons, the Whitakers and the Lyndons. Writing in 1899, George Bernard Shaw could refer to their work as 'rescuing the people of Grayshott from "the barbarism of twenty years ago."' Grayshott at that time was in Headley parish.

The I'Ansons arrived in 1861; the Whitakers in 1884 when Joseph Whitaker bought Grayshott Hall and Wishanger Estate, including the Land of Nod, for one of his sons, Alexander Ingham Whitaker.

Alexander Whitaker was Vice-Chairman of Headley Parish Council from 1894 to 1904, becoming its Chairman in that year and continuing as such until 1908, when he resigned from Headley Parish Council, having become Chairman of the Grayshott Council at its formation in 1902. Thus for four years he combined the two Chairmanships.

Miss Catherine I'Anson also served on Headley Parish Council from 1894 to 1904.

In May 1899 it's recorded that 'a steam roller is in action on Headley & Grayshott roads and Mr Vertue of Grayshott paid to borrow it'.
This photo is from Mr Laverty's collection – could it be the same machine?

Edward I'Anson, 1811-1888.
Bought Grayshott Park Estate in 1861. A family tradition credits him with
having ridden on horseback from Clapham to Grayshott to view the land.
President of the Royal Institute of British Architects from 1886.

Edward Blakeway I'Anson, 1843-1912.
Architect for St Luke's Church, Grayshott.
Founder of the I'Anson Cricket Competition.
Son of Edward I'Anson senior.

Catherine Blakeway I'Anson, 1847-1916, who "almost ran the village of Grayshott (part of Headley parish until 1902) in her time". Daughter of Edward I'Anson senior.

Alexander Ingham Whitaker.
Owner of Grayshott Hall 1884-1928
and benefactor of Headley parish.

Land of Nod, September 1905

Whitaker's car at Grayshott Hall – Registration AA1640 – Aug 1907

Shoot at Land of Nod: Mr Phillips & Mrs MacAndrew, Lieuts Dummer, Humbler, Heppingstone – 8 Dec 1917

Madge Dornville, Harold Lilja, Lt Bloomfield with the Whitakers at Stream, 23 Aug 1918

WISHANGER LODGE

Wishanger Lodge from the lake.

The owner of Wishanger Farm at one time was a William Home but although he had a pack of hounds he became too fat to ride and so he built a lodge to enable him to follow the hunt. This lodge was popularly known as "Billy's Look-out". [*A Frensham History* by Robert Hickling]

Sadly we have no picture of William, but his Wishanger Lodge became home to some interesting people.

In the Headley Directory of 1915, the occupant was George Arthur Harwin Branson. His son, born here in March 1918, was Edward James Branson, father of modern entrepreneur Richard Branson. They moved to Tunbridge Wells the following year (although George's brother James remained in Headley and became a local benefactor).

In their place came Major John Meredyth Jones Evans with his wife Camille. She was Camille Clifford, b.1885, described as "The most famous Gibson Girl ... whose high coiffure and long, elegant gowns that wrapped around her hourglass figure and tightly corseted wasp waist defined the style."

On the following pages are some photos from two of their albums, rescued from being burnt on a bonfire when the Lodge changed ownership.

Camille and her son Robert Victor John, born 27 Dec 1921

Camille turned her back on her past life and dedicated herself to bringing up her son and helping her husband create and run a small farm on the land around Wishanger lodge.

They started with pigs, then moved to chickens, and finally became acclaimed breeders of race horses.

Camille died in 1971 at the start of her 86th year. Her son, the Welsh Guards Captain, Robert Victor John Evans survived her.

Camille with her dogs
and, below, boating on the lake with an unknown lady

Young Robert Victor John with, presumably, his father and friends.

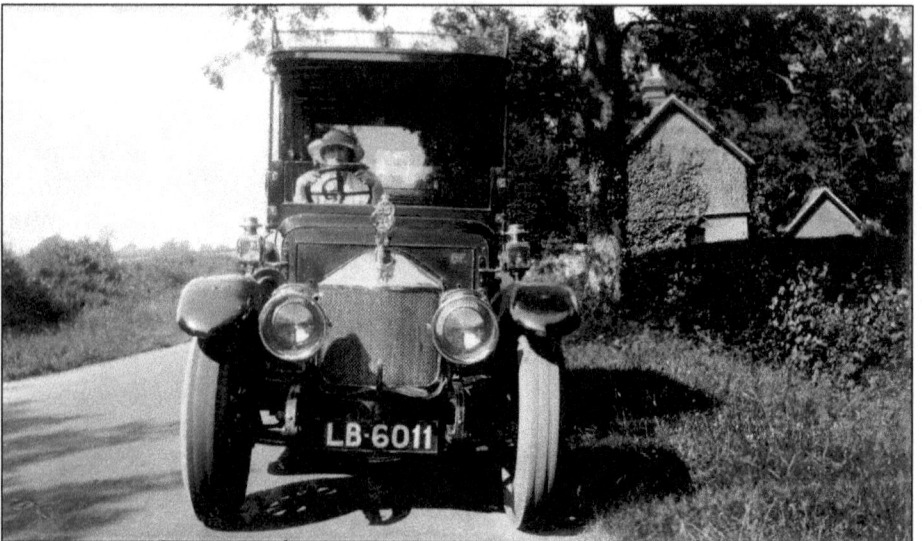

Camille at the wheel, with AA badge prominent.
Note: LB6011 Registered in London between Mar 1908 & Apr 1909

A labour-saving way of mowing the lawn!

"Mechanization: the original Chev lorry with Poulter & Bill Wells"

"The original team: Traveller & Waffle"

No description, but compare with the mechanised version on the right.

How to move a hen house!

Camille doing the work of three horses.

Robert Victor John Evans aged 3.
He became a Captain in the Welsh Guards

WARTIME

World War 1

Herby Hutchinson, a private in the South African Infantry Brigade wounded on the Somme in 1916. He spent time convalescing with people at Brunlea, Beech Hill, Headley. This is him and presumably the lady of the house in the garden. On the back of the original is written "Brunlea, Headley 18/6/17". "My uncle took back to South Africa such happy memories of his times there that he gave the same name to his own home near Durban when he married." [Photo from his nephew, Rowland Hill]

According to Mr Laverty's notes, the lady could be Mrs Wilkinson who came to Brunlea in 1913, or her daughter Blanche.

WW1 postcard showing Frederick Swayne (b.1893) in uniform.
His father Henry is recorded by Mr Laverty as
a "new baker come 1897 to Mr Rogers"
In the 1911 census, Frederick is a 'baker & confectioner'
living with the Tidey family, bakers next to the Crown in Arford.
[Photo from Wendy Buckingham]

WW1 Belgian soldiers who sought refuge in Headley,
photographed outside Hilland. [Tandy Murphy]

World War 2

Lindford section of the Home Guard.
Back row: C Kemp, F Knight, R Harding, J Parker, A Coombs, [?], A Hayter,
E Roke, J Carter – Middle row: C Gale, E Smith, W Wooding, H Shrubb, J
Ellis, L Marshall, F McCarthy, W Souter – Front row: H Davis, J Davis, P
Essex, E Garrett, J Marsh, W Knight, R Viney, E Warner, J White.
[Names supplied by John Ellis]

Members of the Headley Observer Corps.
*Those in the back row were among the first to join. Ted Warner is third from
the left in the middle row. In the centre of the front row is Major General
Twiss who was in overall command. Second from the right in the front row is
canon J Tudor-Jones, then rector of Headley.*

*'The Sewer Rats': Members of the Royal Canadian Engineers
constructing Erie Camp in August 1941. [Phil Herring]*

*Fort Garry Horse regiment in Headley, 12 June 1942.
General Montague with Lt-Col Morton on his left
and Maj EB Evans on his right. On the village green.*

Len 'Henry' Ford talking to boys outside Frensham Pond Hotel, 1941.
He was one of the Royal Canadian Engineers. [Len Ford]

Capt. H Peacey, Lt. John Whitton, Maj. J.H. Wickey, Maj. Bob Grant,
Maj. Alex Christian of the Fort Garry Horse Regiment
in the garden of Long Cross Farm where they were billeted.
Capt Peacey was killed in action on 25 July 1944, and Maj Wickey, who had
served in the Foreign Legion prior to the war, was later transferred to
Special Operations and parachuted into Normandy before D Day
to help organise the French Resistance. [Bob Grant]

Dorothy Ellis on ambulance duty. [John Ellis]
We have in the archives a recording of her memories of wartime work with
the ambulance, including her driving into Portsmouth and Southampton
after air raids there.

PATRICK LAURENCE DUDGEON, Captain, Royal Corps of Signals. Elder son of Lt. Col. C. R. Dudgeon, O.B.E., M.C., and Mrs. Dudgeon, of Beech Hill House, Headley, Hampshire. He entered St. Anthony House in 1934 with a Scholarship. He was Head of the House, leaving in 1938 to enter Woolwich. Commissioned in the Royal Signals in 1939, he volunteered for Commandos, and later Special Air Service, raiding in enemy-held territories. In September, 1943, he commanded a party dropped into Northern Italy, successfully achieving an important mission. With one companion he then ambushed a German amphibian, hoping to reach a further objective. Finally captured near Parma, although in uniform, they were shot next morning on Hitler's orders. He was awarded the M.C., and in 1945 he received a posthumous Mention in Despatches.

'Wings for Victory' parade at the top of Barley Mow Hill.
Cherry Waight is acknowledging the audience. [Cherry Waight]

A group of children at Hollywater, we think taken during WW2.
Back: Ronnie, Gordon, Peggy, Geoffrey, Percy, Betsy Barnett
Middle: Bobby Matthews, Linda Matthews, Elsie Bishop, Eileen Brown?
4 in front: ?, ?, Caroline Matthews, ? Barnett (Renshaw).

MISCELLANEOUS

Miss Birch and Mrs Michell in The Oaks, 1901
[from the Laverty photo albums]

Elsie Mary Caroline Phillips (Mrs Walter Phillips, 1872-1955)
in her small drawing room at Hilland. Album dated 1900.
[Photo from her granddaughter, Tandy Murphy]

Mary Ann Chapman (left, d.1897) mother of Walter Chapman (right).
In July 1901, Walter stabbed his wife Emily to death, was declared insane at
and sent to Broadmoor. Both Mary & Emily are buried at Headley.

Flora Thompson (right) worked in Walter Chapman's post office 1898-1900
in Grayshott and trained Annie Symonds (left) to use the telegraph machine.
She wrote in her book 'Heatherley' about her time here.
Annie (age 16 above) later married Walter Chapman's nephew.
[Photos from descendants & family]

Cherry Waight

Born Cherry Constant in 1899, she remembered seeing Halley's Comet in 1910, and had a flight in an early aeroplane in 1911. She joined the Gaiety Theatre in 1915 and became friendly with Noel Coward. She was one of the first to tour in France at the end of WW1, and later worked in Spain. She married during the General Strike in 1926, and her husband's army career brought her to Headley in 1934. She became well-known in the village for her dramatic prowess, but she was also a self-employed builder (see her card).

She lived to be over 100 years old.

Cherry featured in Vogue magazine

HAMPSHIRE BUILDING

(Proprietor: CHERRY WAIGHT)

THE BARN
HEADLEY, BORDON, HANTS

Telephone: HEADLEY DOWN 2294

*

We Specialise in

COTTAGE CONVERSIONS AND
EXTENSIONS

WROUGHT IRON GATES
GARDEN FURNITURE AND LAY-OUTS

DECORATING
OLDE WORLDE STONE WALLING

Estimates to Serious Prospective Clients

UPHOLSTERY, CURTAINS AND LAMP SHADES

Cherry underneath her tree house – and her business card!

Even lead actors have to make the tea sometimes.

Cherry Waight at 90, in her garden at Alton..

Mrs Kay in 1955, with Cherry Waight's bird 'Jason' on her hat.
The Kays lived at the top of Arford Common in Windmill House,
which was demolished in the late 1960s to create Kay Crescent.

David Hadfield (1925–2010)
Bought Huntingford Cottage and Mellow Farm (then called Lower House)
from Brigadier Evans of Wishanger Estate (see p.99) in 1952
and began mixed farming. He also became a JP, and had a great knowledge
of local history much appreciated by researchers of the parish records.

Margaret Birtles in 2001.
She was chairman of Headley Village Hall Trustees
for 8 years (1972–1981) and involved in many other local activities.

Joyce Stevens in the back garden of 'Suters' in 1999
with the sundial presented to her on retiring as
chairman of The Headley Society

Headley Grange

On 23rd November 1830, a mob of some 1,000 men arrived in Headley having walked from Selborne, and proceeded to ransack Headley Workhouse (now Headley Grange). For this, seven men were transported to Australia – we have a picture of only one of them, Aaron Harding (1789–1851), originally from West Worldham.

There he started a new life with Ellis Packham, had two sons and contributed 18 grand-children and 35 great grand-children to the population of Australia.

Aaron Harding with Ellis Packham and their second child
William, b. April 1848 in South Australia.
[Geof Watts, gt-grandson of Aaron]

The workhouse was repaired, and sold in 1870 to a builder, who converted it into the private house we now know as *Headley Grange*.

A hundred years later, for nearly a decade (1970-78) the house was used as a recording studio where a succession of pop groups came to practice and record their music. The most significant of these recordings is no doubt Led Zeppelin's *Stairway to Heaven*, but the list of bands using the Grange reads like a roll-call of 1970s pop legends and includes Fleetwood Mac, Genesis, Help Yourself, Bad Company, The Pretty Things, Ozark Mountain Daredevils, Clover, Elvis Costello, Supercharge and Ian Dury.

Ozark Mountain Daredevils in 1973.
"While staying at Headley Grange we became good friends with the members of Fleetwood Mac, who at the time were living just up the road at Benifold. All of us would occasionally meet at The Wheatsheaf and share rock and roll stories along with a few pints." [Larry M Lee]

Clover in 1976 – John McFee far right.
"We loved living in Headley Grange! What a beautiful and historic place! We felt privileged to live there." [John & Marcy McFee]

123

Cyril Bloomfield with his wife Ellen (far right) and a representative of Mill Chase School unveiling a 'mural' in Headley Village Hall in the 1990s. Cyril was a long-time chairman of Headley Village Hall Trustees.

Judy Harrold (1928-2001)

A Canadian by birth but very much part of Headley life, many will remember Judy as a Guide Captain with attitude who built a Saxon house in her garden, built log cabins, kept horses & pigs, and played a mean hand of Scrabble.

Champion at Scrabble

Captain of Guides

Breeder of pigs

[Photos from her daughters, Pru and Janet]

Henry Knight (1805–1903)
who, as a boy of ten, remembered
standing outside the Royal Anchor
at Liphook watching the prisoners
from the Battle of Waterloo.

Sir Harry Brittain (1873–1974)
journalist, traveller, MP &
founder of the Pilgrim's Club,
lived at Kirklands *in Arford.*

Joanna Jackson (1915–2008)
(Betjeman's Joan Hunter Dunn*)*
lived her later years in Lynton
Dene, Liphook Road, Headley.

Lady Diana Spencer (1961 1997)
at the Land of Nod in 1978
where she worked for three
months as a nanny.

Sidney Hall at Moor House Farm c.1930 [Edna Morgan, his daughter]

Bridge End, Barford, c.1930. Mr Paterson (in hat) and Frank Thorne with son Frank (peeping over bushes) and his younger brother Raymond.
[Source: Mr Paterson's daughter]

Everybody's
doing it
at Headley Hants

A card of unknown provenance!

List of Celebrities associated with Headley

A-ha, Norwegian pop group – their manager lived in Curtis Lane and Headley post office was their official address for a while in the 1980s.

Baynes (married name Gasch), Pauline, artist whose illustrations for the books of CS Lewis and JRR Tolkien are well-loved landmarks of post-war children's literature – lived in Rock Barn Cottage, the last house in Headley on Heath Hill, the road past Mellow Farm to Dockenfield – died 1st August 2008 aged 85.

Béringer, Oscar, pianist, composer and teacher, lived at Brontë Cottage (they called it Ferrand's Rest) on Barley Mow Hill with his American wife Aimée, the talented writer and dramatist, and his two daughters Vera and Esmé, who became well-known actresses (in Headley c.1913–1935).

Bewsher, Samuel, Bursar of St. Paul's School in London – Crabtree.

Branson, Mrs, whose son James became a great local benefactor – Branson Road in Bordon is named after him. She was also the grandmother of Richard Branson – lived in Wishanger Lodge around the time of WW1.

Brittain, Sir Harry, journalist, traveller, MP and founder of the Pilgrim's Club to foster British-American friendship – Kirklands, Arford (1939–73).

Cecil, Lord Robert, MP, became Viscount Cranborne in 1865 while listed as a resident here at the *Oaks* (now renamed *Cranborne*, bottom of Barley Mow Hill). He later became third Marquis of Salisbury in 1868, and then prime minister both in 1885 and again during the Boer War.

Clifford, Camille – "The most famous Gibson Girl was probably the Belgian-American stage actress, Camille Clifford, whose high coiffure and long, elegant gowns that wrapped around her hourglass figure and tightly corseted wasp waist defined the style" – married Maj. John Meredyth Jones Evans and lived with him in Wishanger in the 1920/30s.

Cobbett, William – visited Headley in *Rural Rides* (1822 and 1823).

Dunn, Joan Hunter (from the poem 'A Subaltern's Love Song' by John Betjeman) – Joanna Jackson lived in Lynton Dene, Liphook Road until the late 1990s – died 11th April 2008 aged 92.

Fauntleroy family at Heath House (Headley Park) in 1600s.

Fauntleroy, Henry – last man to be hanged for forgery (Sept 1824) – Curtis Farm.

Fitzclarence, grandson of William IV. His wife was a Churchill, first cousin to the Duke of Marlborough – first Brigade Major to live at Belmont (1903).

Fleetwood Mac, pop group – Benifold. Lived here 1970–74 before moving to America. In 1969 their recording *Albatross* had been a No.1 hit.

Frankland, Misses and their aunt, Miss Emily Grenside. They were the daughters of the scientist, Sir Edward Frankland – Arford House. Miss Dorothy married Major Richard Hooper and for well over forty years they both took an active interest in the life of the village. Her sister married Mr Woodbine Hinchcliffe.

Gatehouse, Sir Thomas – owned Heath House (Headley Park) during the 1770s and translated the 1552 rent-roll of Headley. His wife Anna Maria (née Huggins, daughter of William, see below) was a talented singer who knew and sang with Handel.

Harte, Brett, an American writer, remembered for his short fiction featuring romantic figures of the California Gold Rush – Arford House.

Hill, Vernon – Little Fontmell, Fairview Road, Headley Down. Artist and sculptor

Hinchcliffe, Woodbine – Pentlow. He designed the Headley War Memorial.

Holme, George – rector of Headley 1718–1765. In 1755, gave the village the school named after him.

Huggins, William – Heath House (Headley Park) – buried in Headley 1761. A literary gentleman who later became a well-known translator of Italian texts, and was a friend of Tobias Smollett and William Hogarth.

Keating, Sir Henry, a celebrated Victorian judge – Headley Park.

King of Norway, **Haakon VII**, lived at *Stonedene* during WW2.

King-Hall, Stephen – Hartfield House, The Hanger. Well-known journalist, political commentator and playwright. Was created Baron King-Hall, of Headley in the County of Hampshire (Life Peer) on 15 January 1966. He died on 1 June 1966.

Laverty, Wallis Hay – rector of Headley 1872–1928.

Led Zeppelin (and other pop groups) – Headley Grange in 1970s.

Lewis, Bunny – Janique and Bunny Lewis owned Peters Barn Cottage (now Winters Barn Cottage) as a weekend home for about 20 years to the 1990s.

Lulu and **Maurice Gibb** (of the Bee-Gees) – Hatch House Farm, Lindford in the 1970s (they were married 1969 and divorced in 1973).

McAndrew, Charles, owner of a shipping line sold to Cunard – Headley Park.

Oland family, later became brewers in Nova Scotia – Grayshott Farm (later Grayshott Hall) in 1861 census.

Spencer, Lady Diana – in 1978 worked for three months as a nanny for Major Jeremy and Philippa Whitaker at the Land of Nod, looking after their two-year-old daughter Alexandra.

Tennyson, Alfred – Grayshott Farm (later Grayshott Hall). He and his family rented the farm in 1867 for about a year while he had *Aldworth* built on Blackdown near Haslemere.

Townshend, Pete of *The Who* – bought Barford Lower Mill (Old Mill) 2006, moved out by 2009.

Van de Velde, Madame, wife of a Belgian diplomat, and daughter of the Italian Ambassador to Berlin – Arford House.

Whitaker, Alexander Ingham – Grayshott Hall.

Wilson, George L, architect of Shanghai – Hatch House Farm 1936–1960s.

Windus, Mrs of the publishing firm Chatto and Windus – Arford House & Kirklands.

Wright, Sir Robert, Justice of the High Court – Headley Park.

Other books from the same Publisher:—

Heatherley *by Flora Thompson*
Her lost sequel to **Lark Rise to Candleford** in which she tells of her time in Hampshire at the beginning of the 19th century after leaving 'Candleford Green.'
ISBN 978-1-873855-29-4

The Peverel Papers *by Flora Thompson*
Nature Notes 1921–27 from the author of **Lark Rise** written while she lived in Liphook. Published here in full and in a single edition for the first time.
ISBN 978-1-873855-57-7

Flora Thompson, the Story of the 'Lark Rise' Writer – *a biography by Gillian Lindsay*
Anyone who has enjoyed Flora Thompson's books will appreciate the opportunity to learn more about this exceptional woman.
ISBN 978-1-873855-53-9

On the Trail of Flora Thompson *by John Owen Smith.* The author of **Lark Rise** lived for nearly 30 years 'beyond Candleford Green' in Hampshire. This book tells of the people and places she met while living locally in Grayshott and Liphook.
ISBN 978-1-873855-24-9

Grayshott *by J.H. Smith*
The history of Grayshott from its earliest beginnings as a minor hamlet of Headley to its status as a fully independent parish flourishing on the borders of Hampshire and Surrey in the 20th century.
ISBN 978-1-873855-38-6

The Hilltop Writers *by W.R. Trotter*
In which we meet Tennyson, Conan Doyle, Bernard Shaw and sixty-three other writers who populated the hilltops around Haslemere and Hindhead at the end of the 1890s.
ISBN 978-1-873855-31-7

John Owen Smith, publisher:—
www.johnowensmith.co.uk/books

Other books from the same Publisher:—

Shottermill, its farms, Families and Mills *by Greta Turner* Two volumes covering the history of this community in the Wey valley from its earliest days up to the start of the 20th century.
ISBN 978-1-873855-39-3
ISBN 978-1-873855-40-9

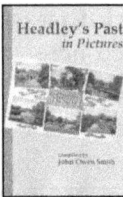

Headley's Past in Pictures *by John Owen Smith* Three illustrated tours of Headley parish in old photographs: in the village centre and Arford; to Headley Down and beyond; and along the River Wey and its tributaries.
ISBN 978-1-873855-27-0

One Monday in November *by John Owen Smith* The Selborne & Headley 'Swing' riots of 1830, their dramatic events and their after-effects are recounted from the known facts and often contradictory reports and legends which have grown up since.
ISBN 978-1-873855-33-1

All Tanked Up *by John Owen Smith* Tells of the 'invasion' of Headley by Canadian tank regiments during WW2, told from the point of view of both Villagers and Canadians. Including details of the regiments involved.
ISBN 978-1-873855-54-6

A Parcel of Gold for Edith *by Joyce Stevens* The story of Ellen Suter, an Australian Pioneer Woman, who fled the poverty of England and set off alone, aged only 19, to live in the new colony of Victoria on the other side of the world.
ISBN 978-1-873855-36-2

A Headley Compendium *by John Owen Smith* Explores authors from John Evelyn and Fanny Burney to H.G. Wells and E.M. Forster. Contains suggestions for further reading and details about places to visit.
ISBN 978-1-873855-62-1

John Owen Smith, publisher:—
www.johnowensmith.co.uk/books

Other books from the same Publisher:—

A History of the Eade Family in Surrey, Sussex & Hampshire (1250–1990) *by Robyn Lane & Andrew Eade* We follow the fortunes of the Eade family over seven and a half centuries, diversifying into trades such as bricklaying and stonemasonry.
ISBN 978-1-873855-58-4

Churt: a Medieval Landscape *by P.D. Brooks*
How our ancestors lived. Philip Brooks mastered the intricacies of medieval Latin to translate and explain the contents of the Winchester Pipe Rolls.
ISBN 978-1-873855-36-2

An Edwardian Childhood, the making of a naturalist *by Margaret Hutchinson*
The family lived near Haslemere – a life of self-sufficiency where the only machine on the farm was the children's toy steam engine.
ISBN 978-1-873855-47-8

Walks Around Headley *by John Owen Smith*
A dozen circular walks around Headley and over the borders, with maps, illustrations and historical notes.

ISBN 978-1-873855-49-2

Walks Through History *by John Owen Smith*
More circular walks at the West of the Weald, with maps, illustrations and historical notes.

ISBN 978-1-873855-51-5

Walks from the Railway *by John Owen Smith*
Circular walks from stations between Guildford and Portsmouth, and linear walks to connect them, with maps, illustrations and historical notes.
ISBN 978-1-873855-55-3

John Owen Smith, publisher:—
www.johnowensmith.co.uk/books

www.ingramcontent.com/pod-product-compliance
Lightning Source LLC
Chambersburg PA
CBHW060310050426
42448CB00009B/1780